Hiking the Vortexes

An easy-to-use guide for finding and understanding Sedona's vortexes

William Bohan

and

David Butler

Table of Contents

Non-liability Statement

The authors have taken every reasonable precaution to make sure that the information herein is up-to-date and accurate. Visits to vortex sites usually involve hiking, and trail conditions frequently change due to weather, Forest Service activity or other causes. The authors and all those involved with the production of this guide, directly or indirectly, disclaim any and all liability for injuries, accidents, and damages that may occur to those using this information. You are responsible for your health and safety while driving to the sites and hiking the trails.

Introduction

If you come to Sedona with the thought of visiting and experiencing a vortex or two, you are certainly not alone. It's estimated that about half of the visitors to Sedona are interested in seeing if they can feel something at a vortex, but many visitors don't know what to expect. By knowing where to go and what to look for, you will have a better chance of having what some call the greatest experience in their lives.

Many people have reported the power and magic at four of Sedona's most well known vortexes (vortices): Airport Mesa, Bell Rock, Boynton Vista, and Cathedral Rock. Included in this book are maps, photographs, and discussions of these four famous vortexes.

Over the years, other Sedona-area locations have been identified as "power spots," beautiful places where people have experienced some form of spiritual replenishment. These include: Fay Canyon; an area near Schnebly Hill Road beside the Cow Pies Trail; the West Fork Trail; and several heritage sites such as the Honanki ruin, the Palatki ruin, and the V-Bar-V petroglyph area, that were central to the activities of the Sinaguan people many hundreds of years ago. All of these well known and not well known sites are shown on the map on pages 10 and 11.

Cathedral Rock

Vortex History

Chicken Point

The Sedona area has always been a special place. The beautiful red rock formations were shaped over the millennia through the ebb and flow of ancient seas, sand, and wind. Geologists tell us that much of the red sandstone in this area flowed into northern Arizona from the eroding Ancestral Rocky Mountains over a quarter of a billion years ago.

Some 11,000 years ago, the Clovis and other hunter/gatherers came to Sedona in search of food and shelter, and a peaceful existence. Even then, native peoples considered the Sedona area a special place and performed their ceremonies under the watchful eyes of the red rocks. At uncounted sites in the Sedona area, petroglyphs etched into the red rocks (some over 8,000 years ago) mark the lives and passage of these early people. Their homes, occupied between 550 and 1400 A.D., are now ancient ruins that still dot the area. Honanki and Palatki Heritage Sites, Montezuma Castle and Montezuma Well National Monuments, Tuzigoot National Monument and V-Bar-V Heritage Site offer the public a glimpse into pre-Sedona life. Various books on vortexes have identified each of these sites as a spiritual "power spot" or vortex.

Although some Sedona old timers insist that there has always been a high level of spiritual energy in this region, it has been only relatively recently —since the early 1980s—that the word "vortex" became widely used.

Honanki Heritage Site

What is Vortex Energy?

People have felt the power of Sedona's vortexes for many years. The term "vortex" is generally credited to Page Bryant who, in 1980, was told by her teacher, Albion, that there are special places around Sedona where the life force of the earth is especially strong.

Albion tried to describe these forces using terms he was familiar with: electrical, magnetic, and electromagnetic energy. It's probably best not to take these terms literally, but rather metaphorically.

Pete Sanders, Jr., proposes that vortexes are not electrical or magnetic at all, but rather are examples of "string theory": sub-atomic strings of particles that exist in ten dimensions and tie the universe together. And while we cannot measure these "strings" with current technology, Dr. Sanders states that they in fact do exist and are responsible for the energy we call vortexes.

West Fork Trail

How Many Vortexes are There
In and Around Sedona?

There's no broad agreement on the total number. Almost everyone with an interest in Sedona's vortexes agrees on the best known ones: Airport, Bell Rock, Boynton Vista, and Cathedral Rock. But many people have proposed that there are other strong power spots. Some of the most often mentioned are:

- Chapel of the Holy Cross
- Chicken Point
- Courthouse Butte
- Cow Pies Trail
- Fay Canyon
- Honanki Heritage Site
- Palatki Heritage Site
- Red Rock Crossing
- V-Bar-V Heritage Site
- West Fork Trail

As you explore Sedona and the surrounding areas, you may encounter certain areas that "feel good." These feelings of peace, harmony, self-awareness and relaxation have been reported at all of the above areas, not just the main vortex sites. Some suggest that because we all have our own unique personalities and life experiences, we "connect" to the Earth at different places, thus resulting in each person feeling the energy and power of vortexes at different sites. So, one of the other power spots in and around Sedona may be the place you feel the vortex energy, rather than at one or more of the four main vortexes.

What Can I Do to Feel the Vortex
Energy?

There are no guarantees when it comes to feeling vortex energy. Try to have no expectations. As you approach each of the vortexes, simply clear your mind and relax. Give yourself several minutes to try to feel the energy coming from the red rocks. Even if you do not think you have felt anything at the time, it is very likely that your being will have been influenced by the energy in ways you cannot yet assess. As the hours and days pass you may begin to understand that you did have an exchange with the vortex. Many people report that they are able to become more in touch with their feelings after visiting a vortex site and many find the peace they were searching for.

What Is The "Y" and What Do I Need to Park at a Vortex?

The directions to the various vortex locations in this book all start at the "Y," which is the roundabout at the intersection of State Route 89A and State Route 179. That intersection is just slightly south of an area known as "Uptown Sedona."

To park on the Coconino National Forest (which is the National Forest surrounding Sedona) at a vortex location, you'll need a Red Rock Pass or equivalent. See Page 39 for additional information.

Where Can I Read More?

There are several good sources that you can consult. One is Dennis Andres' book *What is a Vortex? A Practical Guide to Sedona Vortex Sites* (16th edition, Meta Adventures, 2016). Several earlier books are very informative: Richard Dannelley, *Sedona Vortex 2000* (2001 edition, pub. by the author); Pete Sanders Jr., *Sedona Vortex Information: An M.I.T.-Trained Scientist's Program* (Sedona, AZ: Free Soul Publishing, 1981); and Robert Shapiro, *The Sedona Vortex Guide Book* (Flagstaff, AZ: Light Technology Publishing, 1991).

Some of these books may be out of print, but can still be found on used book sites online. The Sedona Public Library has them all.

Boynton Canyon

Sedona-Area Vortex Sites

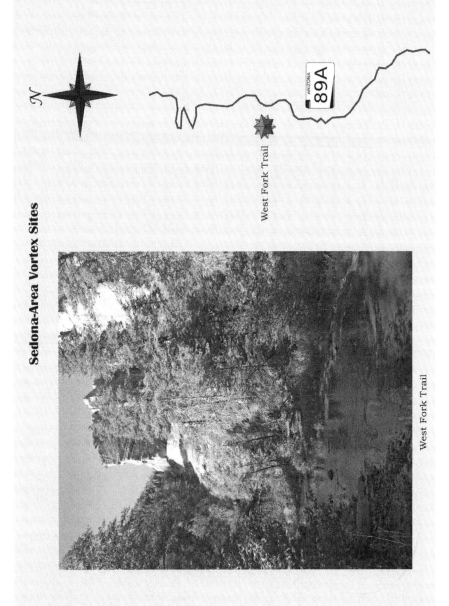

West Fork Trail

West Fork Trail

89A

N

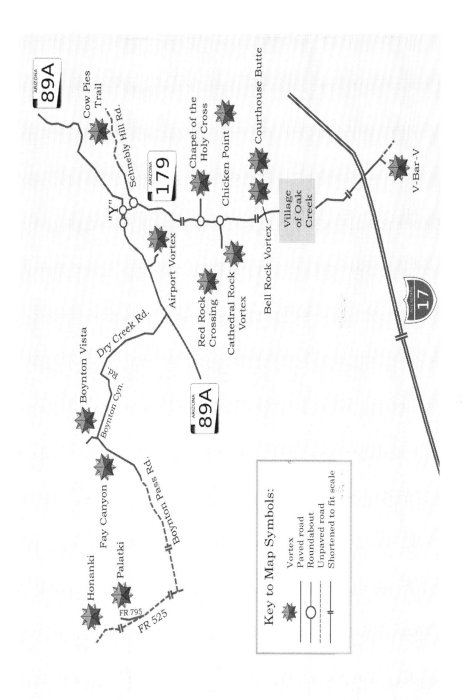

Key to Map Symbols:

✦	Vortex
──	Paved road
─○─	Roundabout
┄┄	Unpaved road
─╫─	Shortened to fit scale

89A ARIZONA

Cow Pies Trail

Schnebly Hill Rd.

Chapel of the Holy Cross

Chicken Point

Courthouse Butte

179 ARIZONA

"Y"

Airport Vortex

Red Rock Crossing

Cathedral Rock Vortex

Bell Rock Vortex

Village of Oak Creek

V-Bar-V

17 INTERSTATE

Dry Creek Rd.

Boynton Vista

Boynton Cyn. Rd.

89A ARIZONA

Fay Canyon

Boynton Pass Rd.

Honanki

Palatki

FR 795

FR 525

Airport Vortex

The Airport Vortex is the most-visited power spot in the Sedona area, probably because it is the most accessible vortex and is closest to the center of town. As you'd expect, you pay a price for this convenience, because you're seldom alone when you visit Airport Vortex. If you'd prefer to avoid the crowds, an early-morning visit is probably for you. Although it will be chilly, even in summer, a visit at or soon after sunrise can be awe-inspiring.

Directions to Airport Vortex

From the "Y" roundabout, drive west toward Cottonwood on State Route 89A for one mile, most of it uphill. As you near the crest of the hill, turn left at the traffic light on to Airport Road. Proceed approximately a half-mile uphill on Airport Road, then turn left into the small paved parking lot, which is located at GPS coordinates 34° 51.345'N, 111° 46.804'W. There is parking for about a dozen vehicles here so an early morning visit will enhance the chances for a parking space.

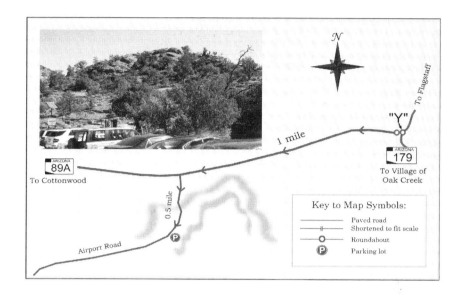

There are many "social" trails (these are paths made by hikers across the land, but not official, maintained trails) between the parking area and the most popular vortex point. To follow the best-maintained trail, turn left (north) about 200 feet east of the parking lot at the marker sign and follow the trail leading to the "overlook." The trail is short (about 0.1 mile in length) but somewhat steep, so watch your footing. The vortex encompasses the entire top of the hill.

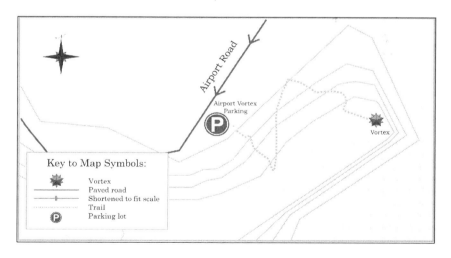

13

Airport Vortex as viewed from the Airport Loop Trail

Airport Vortex as viewed from the Overlook Trail

14

Bell Rock Vortex

All of Bell Rock is considered to be a powerful vortex so the vortex symbol at Meditation Perch is just one of many places you might want to explore.

Directions to Bell Rock Vortex

From the "Y" roundabout, you'll drive south on State Route 179 for about 5 miles to the parking area. After you drive about 3.2 miles, you'll come to the Back O' Beyond roundabout. SR 179 becomes a divided highway just south of the Back O' Beyond roundabout. Continue driving south. About 1.8 miles beyond the Back O' Beyond roundabout, southbound SR 179 adds a passing lane. From the passing lane, turn left at the sign for the scenic view, the Courthouse Vista parking area (it's the second scenic view on the left side of SR 179). You'll see Bell Rock ahead of you on the left side of SR 179. If you continue driving south on SR 179, in 1 mile you'll come to the Bell Rock Vista parking area on your left. But if you park here, you'll need to hike north 1 mile because the south side of Bell Rock is too steep to hike or climb safely.

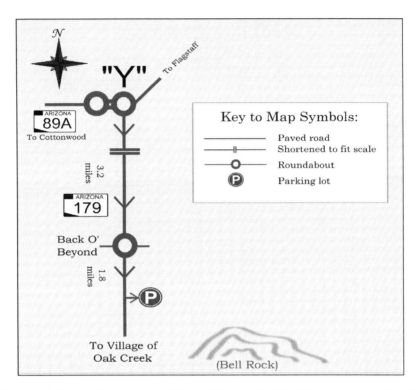

Key to Map Symbols:

──────────── Paved road
───┼──── Shortened to fit scale
───○──── Roundabout
Ⓟ Parking lot

(Bell Rock)

Be careful crossing the northbound lane of SR 179, and park in the trailhead parking lot, located at GPS coordinates 34°48.350'N, 111°46.009'W. The trailhead is on the southeast side of the parking lot behind the interpretive signboard. Before you begin the hike to Bell Rock, take a minute to turn 360 degrees and appreciate the beauty of the area. The Bell Rock and Courthouse Butte area is very popular. You may be able to avoid overcrowded trails by coming to the vortex in the early morning.

There are many paths to explore Bell Rock. After you park in the Courthouse Vista parking area, walk past the interpretive signboard and proceed straight ahead on the Bell Rock Trail. Follow it for 0.1 mile to the intersection with the Courthouse Butte Loop Trail (point [1] on the map). From here you can continue straight ahead on the Bell Rock Trail to explore the northeast side of Bell Rock. Or you can turn right and follow the Courthouse Butte Loop Trail for 500 feet to a signpost on your left. Turn left here (point [2] on the map) and begin climbing up toward Bell Rock. Count the rock cairns along the trail and between the 10th and 11th cairn you encounter, make a sharp right turn (point [3] on the map).

Continue west, then south on the large flat rock shelf. Ahead you'll see where you begin climbing to the Meditation Perch. You'll have to do a bit of scrambling to reach the Meditation Perch, but the climb is worth the effort. This is one of many areas where you might experience the earth's energy as well as enjoy a truly beautiful place. You may see people climbing high up on Bell Rock, but those are people on an athletic pursuit and adventure, not on a spiritual quest. There is no need to climb high up on Bell Rock to have a deeply moving experience.

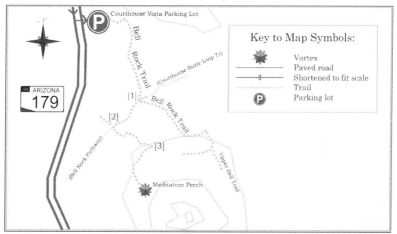

Meditation Perch

Boynton Vista Vortex

The Boynton Vista Vortex is one of the few vortexes you can actually reach out and touch. It is located about 0.6 mile from the parking area and therefore is fairly easy to enjoy. Some say that there are two vortexes on this spot: a tall rock formation to the east known as "Kachina Woman" and a shorter unnamed rock formation to the west. We believe that these two rock formations form one vortex rather than two, but people have reported feeling vortex energy at one and not both rock formations. The number of vortexes here is inconsequential, it is a powerful vortex area.

Directions to Boynton Vista Vortex

From the "Y" roundabout, drive west toward Cottonwood on State Route 89A for three miles to the traffic light at Dry Creek Road. Turn right and drive north on Dry Creek Road for three miles to the stop sign at the three-way intersection with Long Canyon/Boynton Pass Road. Be sure to obey the speed limits on Dry Creek Road as they are strictly enforced. Make a left turn on Boynton Pass Road toward the Enchantment Resort (you'll see the sign pointing left) and follow Boynton Pass Road for about two miles to the next stop sign. Boynton Pass Road continues to the left, and Boynton Canyon Road is to the right. Turn right on Boynton Canyon Road and drive about 500 feet to the Boynton Canyon Trail parking area on your right, located at GPS coordinates 34°54.452'N, 111°50.909'W.

Park your vehicle and proceed through the fence across from the toilets. You'll be following the Boynton Canyon Trail for about 0.3 mile. When you see a sign-in box on a post ahead, look to your right for the sign to the Boynton Vista Trail.

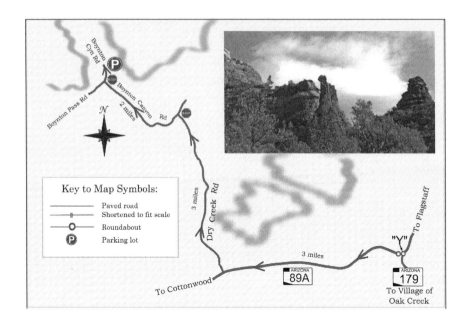

Follow the Boynton Vista Trail for about 0.3 mile. You'll be climbing up about 250 feet of elevation, so the trail is steep in some places. You will see two tall rock formations on your left. These formations are the vortexes. The tall formation on the right (Vortex 1 on the map) is named "Kachina Woman," and the vortex on the left (Vortex 2) is sometimes called "The Warrior." There is a faint trail leading up to the two rock formations. Be careful of loose rock while climbing, and especially while descending.

If you stop and look around Boynton Canyon as you approach the vortexes, you can experience the serenity of the canyon and take the opportunity to reflect upon the beauty. Then climb up the short (but somewhat steep) distance to one of the vortexes. Take some time to rest and calm yourself from the climb up. Then quietly reach out and touch the rock surface. Close your eyes, try to feel the energy coming from the red rock. Don't rush, but give yourself several minutes to try to feel the energy. Next, approach the other rock formation and repeat the process.

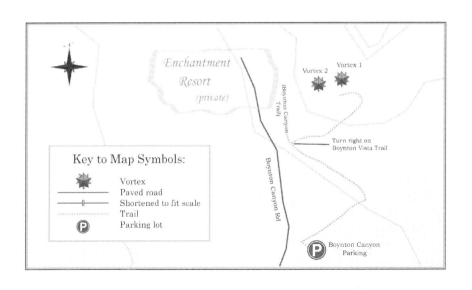

Key to Map Symbols:

✦	Vortex
———	Paved road
—╫—	Shortened to fit scale
··········	Trail
Ⓟ	Parking lot

Cathedral Rock Vortex

The "saddle" of Cathedral Rock is thought by many to be the most powerful part of this vortex, but getting to the saddle involves a strenuous and precipitous climb that is definitely not for everybody. The hike to the "saddle" is only 0.75 mile in length, but rises 650 feet in elevation. It should be attempted only by fit, experienced hikers wearing hiking boots.

Directions to Cathedral Rock Vortex

From the "Y" roundabout, drive south on State Route 179 for just over 3 miles to the Back O' Beyond roundabout. Turn right (west) on Back O' Beyond Road and drive about 0.75 mile to the parking lots on the left. The parking lot is located at GPS coordinates: 34°49.523'N, 111°47.303'W.

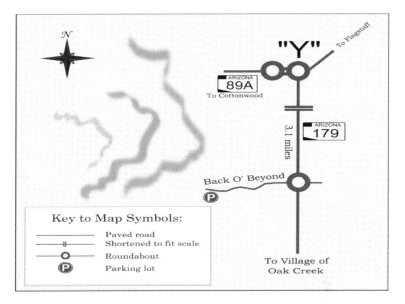

The trail begins on the west side of the main parking area, near the interpretive sign. After crossing a dry creek wash, follow the trail uphill for approximately 0.4 mile until it intersects the Templeton Trail. To hike to the "saddle," turn right and go for roughly 100 feet, where Cathedral Rock Trail turns to the left. From this point to the "saddle" of Cathedral Rock, the trail is one of the most strenuous hikes in the Sedona area. The entire saddle area is considered to be the strongest part of the vortex, but if you would rather not attempt the climb, consider the alternative hike on the next page.

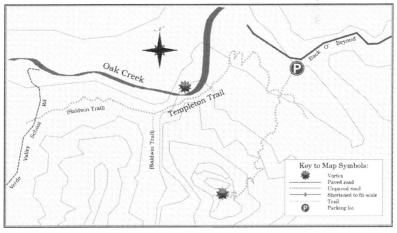

An Easier Alternative Hike to a Beautiful Power Spot

If you would prefer not to hike up to the saddle of Cathedral Rock, take Templeton Trail to the right (west). In 0.7 mile it reaches Oak Creek and then runs alongside the creek.

From the parking area, follow the Cathedral Rock Trail across the dry wash and up hill for approximately 0.4 mile until it intersects the Templeton Trail. Turn right (west) on the Templeton Trail and instead of turning left on to the Cathedral Rock Trail which goes up to the "saddle," follow Templeton Trail around the north shoulder of Cathedral Rock. Proceed down the switchbacks to the wooded area and follow the trail for another 0.2 mile past the switchbacks until the trail runs alongside Oak Creek. Across the creek you will see dozens—sometimes hundreds—of small rock cairns (unless recent high water has knocked them down). This area is known as "Buddha Beach".

Find a comfortable place along the creek to sit, relax, and appreciate the beauty around you.

Some of the older vortex guides maintain that this portion of the creek is a strong and positive vortex area, and many prefer this area over the climb to Cathedral's saddle.

Peaceful Oak Creek, Buddha Beach is Across the creek

Other Sedona Power Spots

The following 10 areas, while not as well known as the four main vortex areas, nonetheless exhibit energy. You may find that you connect with one of these other power spots, rather than one of the four main vortexes.

- Chapel of the Holy Cross
- Chicken Point
- Courthouse Butte
- Cow Pies Trail
- Fay Canyon
- Honanki Heritage Site
- Palatki Heritage Site
- Red Rock Crossing
- V-Bar-V Heritage Site
- West Fork Trail

Palatki Heritage Site

Courthouse Butte Power Spot

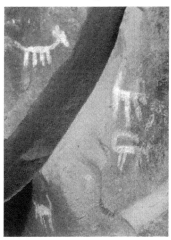

25

Chapel of the Holy Cross

The **Chapel of the Holy Cross** is a facility unique to Sedona. It serves as a welcoming beacon to visitors who enter Sedona driving north on State Route 179. It is a Roman Catholic Chapel which was inspired and commissioned by sculptor Marguerite Brunswig Staude, a student of Frank Lloyd Wright. Through the efforts of the late Senator Barry Goldwater, the Chapel was constructed on the Coconino National Forest under a Special Use Permit. Construction of the Chapel took 18 months at a cost of $300,000 and was completed in 1956.

Directions to the Chapel of the Holy Cross: From the "Y" roundabout, drive south on State Route 179 for 2.8 miles to the Chapel Road roundabout. Proceed 270 degrees around the roundabout and proceed east on Chapel Road about 1 mile to the Chapel. The driveway to the Chapel is steep as is the sidewalk. If you have trouble walking up steep inclines, you should park as far up the driveway as possible. The Chapel is typically open from 9:30 am to 5pm daily; closed Thanksgiving, Christmas, Good Friday and Easter.

Chicken Point

Chicken Point is a vast slickrock area (i. e. a large area of red sandstone that can be slippery when wet or icy but provides excellent traction when dry) that provides expansive red rock views. It received its name from the Jeep drivers, who long ago drove as close to the edge of Chicken Point as they dared. Vehicles are no longer permitted up on Chicken Point; however, you'll encounter visitors on Jeep tours nearby. But that fact doesn't diminish the very positive energy felt by many at Chicken Point.

Directions to Chicken Point: Chicken Point is accessible from the Broken Arrow Trail or the Little Horse Trail. To access from the Broken Arrow Trail, from the "Y" roundabout, proceed south on State Route 179 for 1.5 miles and turn east on Morgan Road. Follow Morgan Road for 0.6 mile to the Broken Arrow Trail parking on your left. Follow the Broken Arrow Trail for 1 mile and turn right at the signpost to Chicken Point. Continue 1.0 mile to Chicken Point.

To access from the Little Horse Trail, continue south on SR 179 for 3.5 miles from the "Y" roundabout and just after SR 179 becomes a divided highway, turn left into the "Scenic View" parking area. Follow the Bell Rock Pathway Trail south for 0.3 mile until it intersects the Little Horse Trail. Turn left and follow Little Horse Trail 1.7 miles to Chicken Point.

Courthouse Butte

Courthouse Butte is considered by some to be a very powerful vortex. The problem is that the power is primarily on the top, which is nearly impossible to get to. There are no hiking trails that scale Courthouse Butte, but there is an area on the northeast side that is accessible and provides a place for meditation.

As you circle on the Courthouse Butte Loop Trail, you'll come to a large rock formation known as "Muffin Rock" or "Spaceship Rock" after hiking one mile. About 500 feet to the northwest of that rock formation is a large area of slickrock, which has expansive views in all directions. It is here that energy has been experienced.

Directions to Courthouse Butte: From the "Y" roundabout, proceed south on State Route 179 for 6 miles to the Courthouse Vista parking area, just north of Bell Rock (see page 15). Park and proceed past the Interpretive Signboard and follow the Bell Rock Trail for 0.1 mile until it intersects the Courthouse Butte Loop Trail. Turn left and follow the Courthouse Butte Loop Trail for 1 mile. Turn left off the trail a short distance to the vortex area.

Cow Pies

It doesn't take much to reach the **Cow Pies** vortex area — only a high clearance vehicle with 4 wheel drive and a short hike. The Cow Pies formation is located close to Schnebly Hill Road, just east of the City of Sedona. Very often you will find medicine wheels constructed from the large lava rocks which are prevalent in this area.

Directions to Cow Pies: From the "Y" roundabout, proceed south on State Route 179 0.2 mile to the Schnebly Hill Road roundabout (just across the Oak Creek Bridge). Drive 270 degrees around the roundabout and proceed east on Schnebly Hill Road. Continue on Schnebly Hill Road for a total of 3.5 miles to a parking area on your right. (Note: after 1 mile Schnebly Hill Road becomes an unpaved primitive road and a high clearance vehicle with 4-wheel drive is strongley recommended.) Park and go across Schnebly Hill Road to the trail. Follow the trail north for 0.1 mile and watch for a large open area on your left.

Fay Canyon

Fay Canyon is one of the prettiest canyons in Sedona. The hike along the canyon floor provides some spectacular red rock views. While the entire canyon has possible vortex energy, the most concentrated energy seems to be near an area known as the Fay Canyon arch. This requires a scramble up the side of Fay Canyon and isn't a hike for everyone. The unmaintained trail up the side is steep and has a great deal of loose rock.

Once you've mastered the climb up the side of the canyon, you'll see a very narrow passageway to the left (north). If you can squeeze into the narrow gap, you may find another dimension as you all but disappear into the rocks.

Fay Canyon Arch

Directions to Fay Canyon: From the "Y" roundabout, drive west toward Cottonwood on State Route 89A for three miles to the traffic light at Dry Creek Road. Turn right and drive north on Dry Creek Road for three miles to the stop sign at the three-way intersection with Long Canyon/Boynton Pass Road. Be sure to obey the speed limits on Dry Creek Road as they are strictly enforced. Make a left turn on Boynton Pass Road toward the Enchantment Resort (you'll see the sign pointing left) and follow Boynton Pass Road for about two miles to the next stop sign. Turn left on Boynton Pass Road and drive to the parking area 0.8 mile on your left. The trailhead is across the road. Hike for 0.5 mile and watch for a faint trail on your right, which leads up the side of Fay Canyon to the arch.

31

Honanki Heritage Site

The **Honanki Heritage Site,** a prime example of early habitation around Sedona, is considered by some to be a powerful vortex area. The Sinagua, ancestors of the Hopi, lived here from about AD 1100 to 1300.

The Pink Jeep Company manages the Honanki (meaning Bear House) site and uses the site for tours so there are no volunteers or rangers stationed here (like at Palatki). You are on your own to wander through the site. There is a metal rail fence to keep unauthorized folks out of the ruins but you are still very close to the structures. Do not touch anything or take anything from the site. There may be people on tours at the time you are at Honanki. The Pink Jeep Company asks that you not interfere with the tours.

Directions to Honanki Heritage Site: From the "Y" roundabout, drive west toward Cottonwood on State Route 89A for three miles to the traffic light at Dry Creek Road. Turn right and drive north on Dry Creek Road for three miles to the stop sign at the three-way intersection with Long Canyon/Boynton Pass Road. Be sure to obey the speed limits on Dry Creek Road as they are strictly enforced. Make a left turn on Boynton Pass Road toward the Enchantment Resort (you'll see the sign pointing left) and follow Boynton Pass Road for about two miles to the next stop sign. Turn left on Boynton Pass Road and drive 4 miles to a stop sign and then turn right on Forest Road (FR) 525. After about 0.1 mile take the left fork of FR 525 (which can be extremely rough) and then continue for another 4.5 miles to the parking area.

Palatki Heritage Site

The **Palatki Heritage Site** is another excellent example of early Native American habitation between about AD 1100 and 1300, and includes both cliff dwellings and pictographs. There are two short 0.25 mile trails at Palatki (meaning Red House): one trail takes you to the Sinagua cliff dwellings, the other goes to the alcoves that shelter the pictographs (painted symbols) and petroglyphs (etched markings) from native cultures who occupied the Verde Valley. The trail to the cliff dwellings has some rock steps and is steeper than the trail to the pictographs. You'll need a reservation at Palatki, which can be made by calling (928) 282-3854. The ranger will ask your name, how many in your party, what day and what time you will arrive (the arrival times are 9:30 am, 11:30 am and 1:30 pm). After you park, walk to the Visitor Center and check in.

Directions to Palatki Heritage Site: From the "Y" roundabout, drive west toward Cottonwood on State Route 89A for three miles to the traffic light at Dry Creek Road. Turn right and drive north on Dry Creek Road for three miles to the stop sign at the three-way intersection with Long Canyon/Boynton Pass Road. Be sure to obey the speed limits on Dry Creek Road as they are strictly enforced. Make a left turn on Boynton Pass Road toward the Enchantment Resort (you'll see the sign pointing left) and follow Boynton Pass Road for about two miles to the next stop sign. Turn left on Boynton Pass Road and drive 4 miles to a stop sign and then turn right on Forest Road (FR) 525. After about 0.1 mile take the right fork, which is FR 795, and then continue for another 1.75 miles to the parking area. After you park, walk to the Visitor Center and check in.

Red Rock Crossing

Red Rock Crossing (which older books sometimes referred to as "Baldwin's Crossing") is a beautiful place where Oak Creek passes close to Cathedral Rock. The afternoon photographs of Cathedral Rock taken at Red Rock Crossing usually feature Oak Creek in the foreground. It is unclear if the vortex energy felt here is from Cathedral Rock or from a source specific to Red Rock Crossing. In any case the vortex energy is powerful here.

Directions to Red Rock Crossing: From the "Y" roundabout, drive west toward Cottonwood on State Route 89A for about 4 miles to Upper Red Rock Loop Road. Turn left on Upper Red Rock Loop Road and drive 1.8 miles to Chavez Ranch Road. Turn left on Chavez Ranch Road and follow the signs for another 0.8 mile to the entrance of Red Rock Crossing. This is a special fee area, so you'll pay $10 per vehicle to enter. Park your vehicle and walk south to Oak Creek. When you come to Oak Creek, you can walk upstream about 0.5 mile to an area known as "Buddha Beach," (see Cathedral Rock Vortex description) where you may encounter many structures made from river rock. Anywhere along Oak Creek has the potential for vortex energy.

V-Bar-V Heritage Site

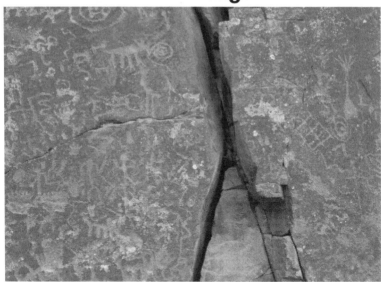

The **V-Bar-V Heritage Site** has the largest display of rock art in the Verde Valley area. It consists of over 1,000 images created by the Native peoples from about AD 1100 to 1300 and whose meanings are not understood.

Directions to V-Bar-V Heritage Site: From the "Y" roundabout, drive south on State Route 179 for 14.75 miles to the intersection of Interstate 17. Drive under I-17 and continue straight ahead on Forest Road 618 for another 2.75 miles. Just past the Beaver Creek Campground, turn right into the parking area, park and proceed to the Visitor Center. The rock art site is about 0.3 mile from the Visitor Center.

West Fork

The West Fork Trail provides an outstanding experience and is perhaps the most beautiful trail in the Sedona area. The tall cliffs of red rocks, babbling water, and abundant flora and fauna over its 3.3 mile length are a treat unlike any other in the Sedona area. As you navigate back and forth across the creek, you'll find peaceful areas for meditation along the way. Vortex energy can be experienced throughout the canyon, beginning as you cross over the footbridge just 0.2 mile from the parking area.

37

Directions to West Fork: From the "Y" roundabout, drive north on State Route 89A toward Flagstaff for 10.5 miles. Turn left at the sign into the parking area. This is a special fee area so you'll pay $10 per vehicle to park here. The trail starts on the far side of the parking area, furthest away from the entrance.

Red Rock Pass Program

When you park on the National Forest to visit a Sedona vortex site, or go for a hike, you'll need a Red Rock Pass or its equivalent. If you park on private property (not National Forest land), you do not need a Red Rock Pass (or equivalent). Red Rock Passes may be purchased at the Forest Service Visitors Center, the Sedona Chamber of Commerce Visitors Center, at many trailheads and at many Sedona businesses.

The Red Rock Pass program began in October, 2000. The Forest Service uses the funds raised through this program for trail and Heritage Site development and maintenance. The Red Rock Pass is available as a Daily Pass for $5 per day, a Weekly Pass for $15, or an Annual Pass for $20.

- The Daily Pass permits you to park on the National Forest for the day of issue. It expires at midnight.
- The Weekly Pass permits you to park on the National Forest for 7 consecutive days.
- The $20 Annual Pass permits you to park on the National Forest for 1 year from date of issue.
- In addition to the Red Rock Pass, there are three Special Fee areas which charge a separate parking fee: Crescent Moon Ranch/Red Rock Crossing ($10), West Fork Trail ($10), and Grasshopper Point Picnic Area ($10). The parking fee for each area is separate.

Instead of a Red Rock Pass, you may display any of the following equivalent passes: 1) a National Parks Pass, also known as a Federal Interagency Annual Pass ($80); 2) a Senior Pass, also known as a Federal Interagency Senior Pass, issued to U.S. residents 62 years of age and older (one-time $10 cost); or 3) a Federal Interagency Access Pass, issued to individuals with permanent disabilities (no cost).

The Red Rock Pass program changes periodically, please check the following websites: http://www.redrockcountry.org/passes-and-permits/index.shtml or http://greatsedonahikes.com for the latest requirements.

Index

Made in the USA
San Bernardino, CA
17 January 2020